for Roy (of the Mountains)
No walker show
on p. 9. A

Nocturnes

WILL KEMP

CinnamonPress
INDEPENDENT INNOVATIVE INTERNATIONAL

Published by Cinnamon Press
Meirion House, Glan yr afon, Tanygrisiau
Blaenau Ffestiniog, Gwynedd, LL41 3SU
www.cinnamonpress.com
The right of Will Kemp to be identified as author of this work has
been asserted by him in accordance with the Copyright, Designs
and Patent Act, 1988. Copyright © 2011 Will Kemp.
ISBN: 978-1-907090-55-4

British Library Cataloguing in Publication Data. A CIP record for
this book can be obtained from the British Library.

Designed and typeset in Palatino by Cinnamon Press.
Cover from original artwork © Blue Forest and Full Moon by
Lorenzo Rossi © agency dreamstime.com
Cover design by Jan Fortune

Printed in Poland

Cinnamon Press is represented in the UK by Inpress Ltd
www.inpressbooks.co.uk and in Wales by the Welsh Books
Council www.cllc.org.uk.

The publisher acknowledges support from Arts Council England Grants
for the Arts

LOTTERY FUNDED

Acknowledgements

Thanks to the editors of journals in which some of these poems have appeared: *Acumen, Aesthetica, Ambit, Dawntreader, Envoi, Equinox, Essence, Fourteen, The Guardian, The Interperter's House, Iota, The Journal, The New Writer, Obsessed with Pipework, Orbis, Other Poetry, Pennine Platform, Poetry Cornwall, Poetry News, Poetry Scotland, Sarasvati, The SHOp, Smith's Knoll.*

Thanks too to Carole Bromley, Ged, Jackie, Doreen, Helen, Ann and Peter Sansom, John Hartley-Williams, Susan Richardson, Jan and everyone at Cinnamon for feedback and fun.

And a special thanks to Sibylle, without whom there would still be darkness.

About the author

Will Kemp studied at Cambridge and UEA before working as an environmental planner in Canada, Holland and New Zealand. In 2010 he won both the Envoi International Poetry Prize and the Cinnamon Press Poetry Collection Award. *Nocturnes* is his first collection. His second collection, *Lowland*, will be published by Cinnamon in 2013.

Notes

Wolf: the quote in italics is from 'The Wolf' by John Hartley-Williams, used with kind permission.

Vienna: after the song by Ultravox, Chrysalis Records, 1981.

Estoril a noite: after the piece by The Durutti Column, Factory Records, 1983.

Contents

I. Night Scenes

II. Night Pieces

*In memory of
my mother and father*

I. Night Scenes

Taking the dog out

The village takes its time to form,
as a clinking chain-lead draws me
into the deep blue paper of the night,
where touches of chalk mark gleaming
roofs, the church's limestone tower.

High above, an arctic moon:
mottled white and oyster-grey, far away
from pub-talk of tax, law, driveways
parked with four-by-fours. It frosts the lane,
limes the surrounding hills and fields.

By a gap in the broken hedge,
Evie inspects her patch—noticing perhaps
those hollow woods beyond the farm,
whitewashed land and barns—then looks
at me to start the way back. But tonight

I step right through, onto a sled
with pelts of lynx and snowshoe hare,
hauled by a pack across this open veld
sloped on either side with dark firs
grazed by elk or caribou, headed for

the tundra of the great white North;
frozen air streams against my face
as we slice over the hushed Mackenzie—
where no salmon leap or drivers holler
above log booms rolling down-river—

whose ice core now shoulders
this ghost rush towards the Pole Star
of an oil lamp by a trading station,
so that only our tracks lead back
to the pale field-hedge, cars and walls.

Wolf

The wolf's howl consists of a single note with up to twelve related harmonics; it rises in sharp crescendo then breaks off abruptly.

You can hear it now, long and low,
        alone,

as the moon clears

and the great unknown spreads out
        in silvered folds,

the frozen lake a star-sprinkled glow,

stalagmite trees pointing north
        like Inuit whalebone spears,

where the shadows seem to move
        with something faint—

but there,

        through the powder snow—

that percussion of panting

        with padded feet.

Forgetting

I forget now the average rainfall in Peru,
the French word for sheep,
that moon in a poem I used to know.

But not that one ballooning
behind silhouettes of leaves, making
silver birches out of all the trees.

We stood in floodlit wheat, listening
to its clicks and creaks. So warm
it could have been Italy or Spain.

The air was sweet, like mown grass.
It shimmered up through a lake of sky
to melt that face beneath the ice.

I likened its white and grey to
oil paint daubed with an artist's knife.
You suggested it was sun-cream.

We laughed. Touched. Kissed.
Then looked at the gaping ground,
which you noted would soon be stubble.

And looking to impress you
with something profound, I said
that the smell of the fields never lasts.

It snowed all night

and no one heard
or saw its fall

in drifts of stars

each flake a kiss
of snow on snow

as soft as silk
waiting to be touched

The woods at Seeheim

After the argument in our snowbound hotel
over what *not* to wear for dinner,
I head for that cool blue air below the moon,

taking the path we came down the day before,
shadows of branches wickering the way,
wind waterfalling through bare tree-tops
where hurried clouds cancel the stars.

Enter a clump of close-set spruce or larch,
extend my arms into the shapeless dark,
slip on ice, send stones tinkling down a ravine.

Lost. Yesterday I knew this track so well,
but now have no idea where to go
or how to get back, unable to read the signs.

Sleeping Beauty

For seven days I hacked into that darkness of thorns,
slashed the briars snaking round my feet, calmed
the horse each time lightning electrified a storm.

Lay awake at night, spooked by the wailing ghouls
whose skulls and armour marked the way, knelt
before the makeshift cross of my iron sword,

praying for their souls. But carried on, thinking only
of the girl who had to be won, the castle inching
higher above the distant trees, until at last

I stood by her bed in its tallest tower, each breath
soft as thread drawn through silk, whilst outside
the snores of guards went sawing through the air.

Sure enough, a blood-clot jewelled her middle finger,
the pillow braided with golden hair. Pictured
her waking: that yawn with outstretched arms,

unwittingly raising the dumpling breasts beneath
her dress – eyes great pools of twinkling blue,
face flushed red at realising a man was in her room.

One kiss and that would be that. Beauty sleep over.
Job done. No need for small talk, frivolous chat.
The most beautiful girl was mine for the taking.

Yet somehow I no longer felt certain. Yes, she was
everything I'd wanted. But didn't know me
from Adam. How could I be sure she was the one –

caring, funny, strong – and wouldn't just fall for
the first man she saw? True, there was her dowry.
I had to think of that. Her face too. A body to die for.

But something in me had changed. I even drew back
to the slit window when she stirred – the woods
below heaving like green wheat in June,

my hard-won path alive with flecks, shadows,
as if a great serpent was sliding towards the walls,
nudging stems as it unravelled. And everywhere,

that crackle. The bushes were prickling back.
In less than an hour, the forest of thorns would have
returned, the groove of my toil sealed like a scar.

All too sharply I could feel those stabs as I lopped
and chopped – this time clearing a path for her
to pass through, perched side-saddle, nose in the air,

heading a mule-train of hat-boxes, dresses and gloves.
Arms folded. Not talking. Until I'd taken back
that plea to roll up her sleeves and get stuck in.

Further down the line too: tantrums, sobs;
not walking the dog. Just wittering on and on
about her favourite pony, how Daddy knew best.

No more dragons to slay, maidens to save;
no fishing on Saturdays, brawls at the inn,
but weekends with the in-laws, tending a cot.

I looked at her, cocooned in another world.
There had to be more to love than this. And
even as the thought was forming, I tip-toed to
the door and left the room exactly as I'd found it.

New Mexico

We head west through the plains at dusk, not a word
since the air-con packed up in Santa Rosa two hours ago.
I shift and squelch in my seat, you hold the wheel
one-handed at its base—which you know I hate, but have
no answer when you say: *Well, whose idea was it to drive?*

I understand now why the cross and beads come
as standard, wonder if LA will be quite this hot, recalling
a lesson on California—temperature, rainfall, that stuff:
Mr Langley on the Sierra Nevada, the San Andreas Fault,
how plants bloom every ten years or so in Death Valley.
I don't think we did New Mexico, but looking at
the map—the Sacramento Mountains, the Rio Grande—

I can see the *campesinos* in their white shirts tilling
the hopeless soil, the horde of bandits riding down
that dried-up creek in pizza sombreros and bullet belts
like windmill slats, heading for some run-down village
where a small boy clangs the iron bell of an old chapel
and dark-haired women rush out to gather in
the uncomprehending children from the dusty square.

Out there beyond the canyon will be a beautiful lady
with sapphire eyes and perfect breasts, cranking
the handle of the ranch's old pump without splashing
a drop on her long blue silk dress; she must put on
Factor Forty every time she goes anywhere and feel
scared at night with all those snakes and coyotes about,

but there's no time to think about that now as I kneel
in the dirt, spitting curses against your mother—
then stop stock-still, squinting at the sun as you stand
in that poncho with a smokeless *cigarillo* and say:
*In this life, my friend, there are those who have guns,
and those who dig graves. You dig, my friend.*

Night Op

The human eye takes up to thirty minutes to adjust to the dark,
at which point it can discern shapes and forms quite clearly.

The gravel scrunched to attention
for Mr Cox's words, faces polished black,
which I hoped would hide my sick fear
of the paras said to be lying in wait
with trip flares and hardened fists.

And now, thirty years on, I can make out
those trees, hedges, woods; see
field after field—blue layered on blue
in a tonal study of distant hills—

though that crack is no fox or cat,
those scarlet dots in the distance
not the power station lights either,
but a pair of night sights on infra-red,
with someone about to pull the trigger.

Out of the darkness

I. Taking the bins out

I pause to look at the stars.
Not that cluster to the left,
or even the shoal overhead,
but those two there, glinting
like coal beyond the woods.

One dot faint and trembling;
the other bright and strong—
a crystal flecked with green
then red like a distant plane
hanging motionless in the air.

Venus maybe, or Cassiopeia.
I've no idea; cannot recall
if either had a little brother
who wondered how on earth
anyone could notice him at all.

II. Stars

like
the   flecks
of   dust
you   saw
as   a   boy
in   that   sunstream

between
the   curtains
and
thought
the   more
you   look
the   more

and
more
you

see

III. Astronomy

Tonight there is no moon,
just an endless spray of stars
splintered from some accident of light
to become heroes, hunters, bears —
or waiting to be named,
as if a stranger to the palace yard
might still stand by its open fire,
beginning such tales of love and war
that even the king would look up
a little open-mouthed.

IV. Harvesting at night

That low hum in the darkness becomes
a chatter throughout this prairie field—

the combine's arm extended like a claw,
long lights floating with corndust stars;

the driver lit up in his cabin too,
as if suspended in mid-air, or peering out

some submersible on the ocean floor,
watching for uncharted wrecks through

a shaken snow-globe of drifting silt,
where a deep sea fish might think him

a lost crustacean searching for a mate—
possibly the loneliest creature it ever saw.

V. Lunar cycle

Only stars tonight,
stones in a bare field,

that mosquito whine
a lone motorbike,

which now lights up
a distant row of trees

like a stills sequence
of phases of the moon.

VI. Night lines

Nightfall
down the lane

silent hedges
wires

a vapour trail
overhead

chalked
across a board

but   fading
      now

returning
        to

the
        thin

dark

        air

VII. Walking back at midnight

In the distance,
a longshore drift of hills,
the rumble of an approaching car.

Its lighthouse beam fans up
behind the crest, then flashes
round to sweep the plain below.

And what you realise
in the stillness of this other world
is the magnitude
of every movement, sound –

that rustle behind a hedge,
the patter of a distant stream –

and the lilac flicker
of those two bedroom TVs
at the settlement's edge,
like signals between ships at sea.

Midnattsolen

not so much sunlight
but cold grey above sweeps of
wind-flattened land

birch petering out
into the silence that is
the endless tundra

its ground cover of
leathery evergreen leaves
scattered with rocks

peat bogs locked in frost
those red dots of bearberries
its other colour

a dead hare a sign
it was surely better
to travel than arrive

Night clouds

The moon darkens
as clouds smoke by
in pale and charcoal grey,

then appears
astonished

at the village below –
soldered roofs,
snow-blue roads —

but now returns
to the night,

sky closing in
like pack-ice
across the Beaufort Sea.

Beckwithshaw

Above the night-charred branches
of bare ash trees

a flurry of orange clouds
as if the sky had been switched on

or somewhere far away
a city was burning to the ground

The end of the world

I am last at the office tonight, about to ping
a draft final report into the abyss of cyberspace.
The rows of desks have been left as they were,
the phones completely quiet, dead perhaps,
as if I was the sole survivor of a nuclear error,
all my colleagues vapourised in a cloud of dust.

Shortly I will leave for the car park, recording
my time of departure in the book on reception
like an entry at a funeral, then step out onto
the wet, still lit street, where there will be
no policeman on his beat, no smokers hunched
like conspirators outside The Wig And Mitre.

Without another car in sight, I will drive past
the outskirts of this northern town, stopping
at the garage for the milk you need for a cake,
helping myself to as much Premium Unleaded
as I like—and maybe some Mars Bars, crisps,
papers and barbeque charcoal since I'm at it.

Clutching my stash in one hand while waving
to the security cameras with the other, I will
at last head home—though starting to see now
the door will not open to KD Lang or Handel
playing throughout the house, nor will there be
any hint of the spicy noodles you had for lunch,

because this is the end of the world—that time
prophets with long beards and shaking fists
always said would come: no point in anything
anymore, everyone gone. No mug by the sink,
no note on the fridge; no chance either to ask
how your day was, or even say good-bye.

II. Night Pieces

Swan Lake

I wake at four, right arm dangled artfully overhead,
left foot behind the other knee in a horizontal pirouette,
as if I had not lain awake half the night fretting
over the job and pension, but dreaming of ballet.

Perhaps it is just my body telling me to quit—
that instead of walking into the office after nine,
I should carry on to the School for the Performing Arts,

where I will stand in a great room walled by mirrors,
a middle-aged man looking lost in a white leotard
among the nine year old girls wearing fairy tu-tus,

then strain not to topple over while balancing on one leg
as an elderly lady plays a jangling piano from behind
her specs, and another stamps a walking stick
on the wooden floor, shouting, *Andante, andante!*

No longer will I see my sagging jowls or the paunch
that passes these days for a mid-riff, but the gaunt tone
of a gymnast who must live off a diet of mackerel
and spinach to glide swan-like over the silent boards,

so that all remains of my occupation, whatever it was,
is the series of taunts I will suffer each night
from my former colleagues on the way to the station—

an ordeal I will come through perhaps by thinking
of the framed photos that will now adorn the lounge—
that bow at Covent Garden, those flowers at the Kirov,

and the one of which I'm definitely most proud—
arms flung wide, head thrown back—
as I take off in a great leap of tighted legs
through the spotlight of an otherwise darkened stage.

Night-pieces

Some Chopin or Satie helps,
my mother's rice-paper lampshade too,
these sketches from my notes.

Fragments, mostly — tabs I've kept
or jotted down to get back to sleep,
clueless where they'll take me.

Here, for instance, a pondered scene:
the china roses of moonlit clouds,
semi-tones playing in a different key.

And here, the moon floats away,
lost in a dream, then plays ping-pong
above the zebra stripes of trees.

Some distillates I like the sound of —
lambent, opaque — with *luminescent*,
a word made up by mistake.

Grand designs, too: that poem
headed *The Dark Side of the Moon*,
abandoned like an old lead mine.

And this one called *I lost my heart
to a girl with parents from the planet Zog*.
After all these years, still just a title.

Vienna

Walked in the cold air

freezing breath in a headlit stare
steaming and waiting

your face pale in the dark
a Russian spy
now closing towards me

that crystal look
as your eyes shut
and we kissed for the first time

*

I began the way home

tints of frost on the side-verge grass
touched by a snow queen

maybe the daylight would bring
a cool empty silence

the warmth of your hand fade
to the distance

*

but what did I care

on my black iron bike
in the middle of the night

a king of the Steppe
riding a Cossack horse
over the silent white of the Volga

Estoril a noite

At the end of the journey,
we walk along the esplanade
between dimly lit bars
and the darkness of the sea.

Small waves hush the shore,
as somewhere by the Rua Direita,
a guitar plays *saudade*,

its notes twisting up
past shutters, roof-tiles, stars,

while an old man pauses
from a game of cards
to recall the one
he loved and lost and longs for.

Orpheus

after Paterson after Rilke after Ovid

In the forest, a clearing
steeped in light.
And at its centre, seated,
a man, head bowed.
All was still.
And then he touched the lyre.

One by one they came,
from every fox-hole, nest and lair,
not drawn by scent,
or out of fear or stealth,
but the sound
of slow notes pouring through the air.

Without a growl or snarl,
they sat about the ground—
lion, vixen, deer—
each looking down
with eyes that knew his loss,
and understood now what it was to feel.

Nocturnes

I. Chopin

I step from the French windows,
the sky a mine of stars,

the garden lit by an upstairs window
like an audience in a cinema,

its silence the same as before

that first faint note
    of Chopin's Ninth Nocturne,

        the pause too
            leading into the next,

            then falling
                    to a third,

                slow as the plink of droplets
                    from the roof

                    gathering into a trickle,

as if he sat at a Steinway Grand
in the lounge, hand gliding over hand,

a ripple about the long curtains,

while the notes drifted into the dark
to present the night with itself.

II. Clair de Lune

I see Debussy
at the keys

pausing
to note

the mottled form
and muted tone

of those snowdrops of light
outside

as a full moon
blanches

the stone slabs
of the garden path

and a slight wind
skitters some leaves

this way
and that

then gently
falls away

III. Arabesque

What did Debussy have in mind
when he wrote this piece?

A fountain perhaps, tinkling
in a palace yard under the stars.

Or a new-born foal
just struggled to its stilted feet.

These doves even, caged
in my mother's old Persian rug:

one singing a trill lament
as the other preens herself in a tree

then hops down to another branch
and warbles back,

ready to play hide and seek
among its flowering leaves.

IV. Gymnopodie

In the distance, the notes of a Bechstein
are stopping on the evening air,

as if joining the dots of a picture
that becomes a *fin-de-siecle* couple

taking a stroll towards a Monet bridge,
the August light still not fallen,

each composed step leading to
a slight swish of that long linen dress,

a white parasol opened behind the bun
of brown hair above her high collar

as she takes in the willows, water-lilies,
that fragrance of French Lavender,

whilst her suitor in a Panama adjusts
his cravat to ask if she too considers

the full orchestra an *ensemble de trop*,
for her to blush a little then say, *I do.*

V. Eine Kleine Nachtmusik

How soothing the flow of strings, especially
this piece pouring through the house,
its first three notes a little *staccato*, delayed,
as if sending a telegram to another age—

the Edwardian era perhaps, or shortly after,
when we might have stood on the upper deck
of the Titanic as it started to list—

not joining the melee by the lifeboats,
the scrum at the bar with drinks on the house,

but looking up at the moon one final time
to note the silvered calm of the water,
the dark blue depth of the sky,

and the string quartet that chose to play on,
as if this might restore some decorum,

so that for a moment we recalled the time
we met at that ball for your sister Lavinia,

and then as now, quite forgetting myself,
I offered my arm to your long satin glove
for the honour of this last dance,
and said how beautiful you looked.

VI. Moonlight Sonata

The night you ended it,
I found the tape of you playing

your father's grand piano –
muffled, *sotto*,

each note a spider's step
in case he told you to stop –

less a reminder of that moon
we watched,

dawning above
those distant woods and fields,

than the town hall clock
on our first date,

iron hands like garden shears
clunking back to twelve.

VII. Gnossienne

If you're sitting alone, through with love perhaps,
wanting the darkness to end, then this may
not be the best thing to play right now,

least of all this recording—distant, slow,
maybe made over a century ago, a pianola echoing
down an empty hall, from an empty room,

its brittle chords returning like waves that roll on
and on to the shore then fold into the beach
with the monotony of a chanted prayer,

making you feel you're the last person on earth,
staring at the flat skyline beyond the sea,
nothing more to do than move off across the sand

into the one world left at your feet,
no longer thinking about the whorling wind
or the note left behind that nobody will ever read.

III. Night Thoughts

After dinner

we sit back by the table with a bottle of wine,
the candle fluttering like a wind sock—
me peering at its wax stem,
smooth as an omelette, thinking
how it stands above the dark napkins
like a column in an excavated forum,
you still pondering van Gogh:
did he owe his style more to Monet or Renoir?

I don't know, wondering now if someone
will ever ask about your shepherd's pie,
the one you do with mushrooms and thyme,
whether it owed more to Jamie or Delia,
if the flavour of your salads was due to
the selection of seasonal leaves
or the mustard and lemon dressing
you have made your own,
a signature only discernible to
distinguished connoisseurs of your works.

People with such taste would never scoff,
but rather observe each meal
as a statement of your under-stated genius,
then single out your apple crumble,
the one you did tonight even,
its crust of crushed almonds
an unnecessary touch perhaps,
but the custard so warm and sweet
it would cruise into a documentary
on the hundred greatest things,
or a guide on how to take away
the emptiness at night.

Halloween

What a relief I am not at home tonight,
opening the door with that surprised smile
to gangs of small children demanding money.

How preferable to be sprawled across the sofa
in a holiday cottage in the Dales, nothing
more troublesome than figure out how
to work the remote, where to find a corkscrew.

Here, there are no grinning pumpkins
or ketchup-stained kids roaming the streets
in vaudeville masks, jokeshop outfits—
Dracula, Frankenstein, Hannibal Lecter—

no parents either, looking on with pride,
expecting some kind words on the wit
and originality of their little horrors.

No need to switch off the lights then cower
in the bathroom until I'm sure they've gone,
still expecting the letter-flap to open
with that call, *We know you're in there.*

Better to listen to the owner's collection
of *Music in the Forest* CDs, or read her copy of
I Lost My Heart At Wounded Knee,

than stand speechless in the hell of my porch,
facing rows of glow-in-the-dark teeth,
unsure if a pound each would be too much,
or not enough to make them go away.

Lying awake at 4am, I consider the social and physical characteristics of hell

The darkness much the same, but with a red glimmer
on the cliffs where the new arrivals are bull-dozed off
by rat-faced demons from a work by Hieronymus Bosch.

It comes as no surprise to see the neighbours here,
my lawyer too, thriving amid the sobs and cries of woe,
though I could do without that welcoming party of MPs
extolling the rewards and virtues of hard work.

And for that matter, colleagues I tried so hard to like,
three women on a hen-night, peeing in the street,
some hippies singing peace songs round a camp-fire —

because this is hell: orange rivers of molten rock
and searing flames—no need to light another fire at all.

No dogs either, no trees or sky. Just the black smoke
of burning tyres rolling across deserts of ash, basalt rock,
where the damned stoke vast furnaces then trudge
down dead-end streets to a deluge of Saturday night TV.

No small comfort, then, to behold kings who founded
great abbeys to pray for their souls, the father of my ex—
still shouting—a board on his back saying, KICK ME.

Which makes me think, maybe there is a God after all.

Insomnia

What to write on statutory strategic spatial planning
and infrastructure capacity in the draft annual report;
that Sibylle always has the lion's share of the duvet.
Everything I didn't say about the scale and distribution
of hazardous waste facilities to the Planning Inspector;
if England should play a spinner against South Africa.
The need to read Sean O'Brien and get my head round
the revised funding criteria for transport schemes,
taking into account the settlement network hierarchy
and public sector squeeze—our top priority according to
the Chair of the Sub-Regional Spatial Planning Board,
despite saying much the same about urban regeneration
and climate change at each of the last three meetings.
How many fish begin with the letter H; why did I get
nowhere with Debbie K. Some mineral operators'
objections to revised aggregates apportionments;
how cold it must have been for those polar explorers.
Where to get funding for work on renewable energy;
what bad breath people must have had for centuries.
If I sleep worse in winter or summer; finding a joke
to open a presentation on flood risk in the Humber.
That I have no idea on types of employment land
in North Lincolnshire; how scientists must have found
so much fruit is eaten by the Madagascan Lemur.
Whether development will become a free-for-all
if the Government loses power; the need to postpone
the Easter holiday until the service review is over.
Whether I should go back to consultancy, or teach;
that Evie's paws will be twitching as she chases
a rabbit in a dream. How I can establish if drainage
refers to foul or surface water without fear of ridicule;
what I'd like to tell Sventje's father but never will.
Things to add to a new list of things to do, and
the poem I must remember to write in the morning.

Evie

Let me not believe it is sentimental to love dogs.
Rather, let me watch Evie sleep, a wolf-bear
lost in dreamworlds of cat chases and juicy bones,
paws twitching, tail thumping against the floor.

Let it be me who has just appeared in that dream,
throwing a stick or walking through the door
so she leaps up then skitters round the lawn
three times in wild disbelief that I am home.

Rather than think dogs have no feelings, let me
kneel to hold her when she sits looking down,
or curl up on the floor to tickle that tummy spot
which makes her back leg pedal in the air.

Let me never throw away her doggy toys—
the rubber ring, the squeaky chop—or turn back
when she runs ahead, finding some patch
to sniff—but really checking I'm still behind.

And when the time comes for her to go,
let me just be there, stroking those silk ears
and saying she's a good girl, watching over
her the way a father does his sleeping child.

Night Thoughts

I. Nightfall

Not dusk,
or even its pale blue after-glow
shoring the top-heavy dark,

but night itself,
silent, unformed,
stretching beyond Venus, Mars,

sprinkled with frozen light
and all the thoughts
still left from the past.

II. Sky

I touch the page,
uncertain what to write.

The pen knows
this is not a good idea—

late at night,
the window open,
only darkness outside—

but then begins
with a distant train,
that sickle of a moon,

as I recall
the time as a child
I stole from my bed
to the glistening lawn,

and stood barefoot
under that enormous sky,
looking up
in silent amazement
at all the stars.

III. Tonight

the sky is deep
and far away.
No wind, clouds,
no sound at all.

So few stars,
like camp-fires
dotted across
a desert plain.

And that blue:
glacial, smooth,
the same as each
night at school,

when you stood
by that window
looking out
north-north-east,

where your mother
sat alone by
her china lamp,
writing the letter

to arrive the day
after next,
as if kissing
you good-night.

IV. Night thoughts

The moon locks the garden below
in metallic grey: flint leaves,
steel grass, glittering with frost.
As if I watch through tinted glass.
A lost world. How much smaller
the lawn than the one I knew
as a boy. Shrub borders tapered it
like a map of England: a willow
by the Humber, that stone sun dial
we used as a wicket outside Bristol.
My mother's design. I see her
bringing out scones and milk, hear
my sister Liz calling us to look
at cartwheel after cartwheel.

V. Lumiere

newly
slit,
you're a
sabre in
silhouette,
a toe nail
tip, an
oyster
in its
shell.

cut to
D, you're a
slice of lemon,
or leftover pie, a
face obscured from
view, a snake's
half-opened
eye.

hole-
punched, you're
a peep-hole in the sky,
a snowball turned to
stone, the pearl a
diver gives his
girl.

VI. Spatial Planning

The career I've come to know:
assessing future housing needs,
how places handle
energy, waste and transport.

People struggle with the term,
especially my sister—that clouded look
even after twenty years,

as if I determine the orbit
and axial tilt of planets,
each evening draw down
the last blue of daylight,

then arrange the coalescent stars
like a cluster of satellite towns
or a night-shot of Europe's streetlights.

VII. Last night

I sat in my room, too tired to sleep,
an ice-flow of moonlit clouds

giving way to candlelit stars
massed in that endless royal blue.

No wind flailing the bare trees;
no streetlights, browns or greens.

Only marbled gardens, fields;
the road an iron river over the hill.

And the thought that if I sat
by an open window, watching

my very last sky, then that one
would be just the kind I'd choose.

Fountains Abbey

You would love
the ruin now—
its frosted lawns
and flame-red beeches,
that yew a steadfast green.

You would know
how there must be green
with red and gold,
find similes for leaves,
think nothing of it too.

You would pause
by the great arch window,
liken its shards of stone
to a shark's jaw
mounted on a wall.

You would ask
if I had a dog,
a house, a garden,
was I playing cricket,
had I found another girl.

You would see
the place in snow,
hear those rooks caw
from the tower, dark
against the evening sky.

You would look
at its pink and blue,
ask me to do so too,
then say it was time
we were going home.

Room at the top

The boiler fires into life upstairs,
causing me to see my father as a boy
sitting alone in his attic room,

a paraffin lamp guiding
his study of algebra, Latin grammar—
the table bulked with library books,
that copy of *Pilgrim's Progress*
which used to belong to his father.

No bother to him the bitter grit
of that black air, or the shunt and clank
from the marshalling yard by Oswald Road,
as an engine strains uphill out of the smog
with truck-after-truck of coal
for the smelting works at Frodingham.

And no wonder he would later turn
to me with his father's words—
that there is always room at the top
for pure excellence, *but getting there
is like the long haul of a goods train through the night.*

After my father died

I sat on the bed in my shorts and vest
the way he would sometimes do,
an ocean of darkness outside.

His laboured breathing still there
from the afternoon, times too he taught me
how to ride a bike, swim, bat, pee—

or recalled flying bombers in the war,
his vow to marry my mother, getting into
Cambridge from a northern grammar.

But never the Depression before:
people laughing as he shovelled droppings
behind a cart loaded with scrap,

his dad with the reins, always coughing;
all working back to the morning
it stopped—news he was told

in front of his class—the allotment shed
spattered with blood, the note
he was never allowed to read,

and what he must have felt going to bed
that night, the dark sky without a star,
a boy in a world all at sea.

Night flight to Frankfurt

We move through the night, a calculation in distance
over time, with variables of velocity, thrust and fuel.
The engines steady, no longer that whirlwind roar
at take-off—flare-white flashes from the undercarriage,
the runway's amber dots zipping by like tracer fire—

the same colour as the streetlit settlements of Holland
below, which glimmer like fissures in a lava flow
cooling to a mass of black rock, clouds drifting by
like dissipating steam. Something my father
wouldn't have seen as a young navigator faced with

his first mission, yet this is the route he trained for:
east-south-east to Arnhem, the moonlit wire
of the Rhine and the Ruhr, the drop-zone over Köln,
heavy flak coming up around Essen. No practice runs
anymore; no leg-room either, or an automatic pilot

to find a way through the dark—just checks of altitude,
windspeed, bearings on charts. No wish to put up
a good show, or teach Gerry a lesson, but get home
without Messerschmidts at two o'clock, ice jamming
the tail-flap. And all the time wanting nothing more

than to sit back as I do, above an Autobahn joining
the pearls of a Ringstrasse—where people will soon
be walking their dogs, children going to school—
the pale lights of some city rising in the distance
like dawn, instead of a smouldering ruin.

Thinking of Holland

I. Memory of Holland

translated from Herinnering aan Holland by Hendrik Marsman

Thinking about Holland
I see broad rivers
drift through
endless plains,
rows of such
thin poplars
as tall as smoke plumes
far away;
and sunk within
that peopled space,
scattered farms,
woods, villages,
willow towers,
churches and elms
as one great whole.
the sky is low
and the sun slides
into a fuming mist
of different greys,
and in every province
the voice of the water,
with its disasters
long since passed,
is still heard and feared.

II. The things you gave me

I still have the things you gave me,
hidden in a secret place.
Letters tell how we used to be,
photos let me touch your face.

Hidden in a secret place,
an old tape brings back the past.
Photos let me touch your face,
the poems you wrote let love last.

An old tape brings back the past.
Letters tell how we used to be.
The poems you wrote let love last.
I still have the things you gave me.

III. The light on the water at Rhenen

It was a Saturday in July—
the sky pale but open wide;
typically Dutch, you said,
an unhurried cloud passing by.

We sat on rough grass,
you in my sweater, if I remember,
bicycle wheels still spinning,
ticking, by the water's edge.

The river slapped and plopped
again and again. Further out,
it seemed to glitter silver
the way leaves do after rain.

We watched a *kahn* inch forward,
lugging coal to Koblenz or Köln,
a line of shirts in surrender
from bridge to stern.

I put my head on your lap,
you fed me apricot Limburg Flan—
but only after I'd said
sinaasappelsap.

You explained polders, dykes,
the need to maintain the water level.
I kept quiet about the way
your father looked at me that morning.

I once heard that every life
has a point before which there is
always a looking forward,
afterwards a looking back.

These are the things I think of,
whenever I think of that.

Afterwards

I pull in, on the verge
by a sign for Leiden;
a name you might have given
to a cat or character
in the novel you never wrote.

Ahead, bare fields, a wood
we could have walked in
or made love,
that late sky a shroud
the low sun almost breaks through;
and high above,
a vapour trail that unzips
the blue then vanishes into thin air.

According to the priest,
who confessed he didn't know you,
you're there.

God knows
I want to believe him—
that it's you in that distant hum
of a microlite, the V of a raven
slipping away beyond the trees
and out of sight.

Instead you remain below,
in boxed-up books and clothes—
Sylvia Plath, your velvet top—
a laugh from that day by the river,
and all the things I didn't say or do.